I can't stop
drinking about ~~you~~

Foreword

As God as my witness
I knew when I said
"I Loved You"
for the first time
I just didn't know
what it meant

As our love grew
I couldn't help but smile
I was so blessed
to be part of your life
even if it was for a while

You taught me what it means
to be a man and a boy
at the same time

No words
no actions
nothing at all
could ever describe
how special
you are to me

If the world could see you
as the angels do
and as I truly do

People would believe in forever.

-Brandon Villasenor

The flower in your hair
was combined
with the aroma in the air
thought about what to say
instead just stopped and stared
as you walk through the hall
I became impaired;
thought I seen it all
turns out
I was blind all along

If you ever need a reminder
I'll always be the boy
who held your binder
who held your hand
cause I knew your heart
was just a little bit kinder

the boy who walked you home
so you didn't have to be all alone
who left you paragraphs
messages on your phone

you were perfect to
your face to your feet
listening to you speak
my knees became weak
we literally couldn't stop
kissing for two weeks

hypnotized
by the way
your skin felt
the way the sun melts

Now I know those days
have long past but
If you ever need a reminder
I'll always be the boy
who held your binder

The first day of school is when I noticed your smile
so beautiful I noticed it from about a mile &
don't even get me started about your style
it drives every boy in town wild

That day my life would never be the same
one glance at you I knew our child's name

When you were leaving math class
here's what I've been meaning to ask,
I've felt this for quite some time
& I know baby you must be mine
so here's what I'm trying to ask
can I have your hand &
I promise our love will last

Stayed by the locker
talked until the world got awkward
let me take your book and walk you to class
I know we're late but with me you'll always have a pass
as we walked toward class
along there was some fresh-cut grass
you held my hand & we began to laugh;
The sun was melting your skin
the way you moved in those moccasins.
You pulled my hand & we started to sprint
saying "come on, class in about to begin"
We raced throughout the whole school
watching her air in the breeze I was forever a fool
I could go on & on about this girl but
the bottom line is that I found a jewel;
people say money makes world go round
but once you know this girl you know
the very meaning of love was found
This story ended many years ago
my love and scares "Yeah" they still show
but just like all streams flow to the open sea
We'll be together
Because your hearts a lock
& I'm the only one with it's key

I can't stop drinking about you
my pen and paper will speak
louder and truer than
my lips ever could do

As this ink spills on my shirt
as this rum fills our hurt
remember when my hands
felt up your skirt
I know you remember
because I was the first

There's a space that only you can fill
I love you then I always will
I still feel those midnight chills
Thinking about the moment until

The waterfalls run down your eyes
as it drips into my heart
My love is never fulfilled
because you have the other part

I still sit here & play my guitar
strum ever string
tuning to the sound of who you are
singing all alone at the bar
my drink can only take me so far

I thought of you in a puff of smoke
I drank my ways & danced to folk
I wrote ever word you forgot in that
Final Note

Intertwined

You're naked in sunlight
wrap yourself up
& goodnight

Squeeze my hands
as our lips tight
sing your song
as my heart drips wine

Unless fine lines
undress my demise
as I'm making your body die
remember how much our skin
completely intertwined

Exquisite

I'm in love with a girl named sin
she kisses me when the lights so dim
she's my pleasure
when my fuses
are burning thin
so I'm forced
to catch a glimpse

Lord forgive my sin
for I'm about
to indulge
in her
exquisite
skin

You let your demons run a muck
you scream at heaven
cause your life's stuck in a rut
what do you think happens
when you treat your soul like a slut
your friends tell you
"drink and party who gives a fuck"
guys call you at midnight saying
"Heyyy whats up"
hasn't your body had enough
open your heart & keep your legs shut;
you've indulge in every single drug
every fake friend hug
It gets to the point when your tears
turn into cuts
you're a volcano ready to erupt;
you crave something real
you feel it in your guts.

But let me tell you something
something you've never heard
a man died for you because
he gave you what you already deserve
A place in paradise a destiny reserved

You have deep wells of strength
& oceans of love
overcome this world and you shall
inherent glory from above;
I love you too much to say goodbye
I can't remember all the words that I said
but I shall remember these instead

"You're my love you belong in my arm's laughing & smiling in my bed".

The
purpose
settles
on the
pedals
of your
surface

My love
made you
nervous

I
wonder
if
his
is
even
close
to
perfect

Ice Cream

I press my hands up
To the bricks around your heart
Grasp my palms
Use my strength to tear them apart;
One brick turned into three &
Eventually Until you couldn't even see
That beautiful girl who use to climb trees
& smile at ice cream

I know It's been so many years
& your joy is drained in tears;
But hold my hand & watch the world close its ears
as you scream into the face of fear
Scream! Scream!
Until your life's no longer a bad dream
& you can finally enjoy
your fucking ice cream

Every Eyelash

As the moonlight escapes

in-between your eye lashes

Every blink I realized the pools of joy

that you were begging me to splash in

Every eyelash fell gracefully on your cheek;

you slipped sex into my mouth and told me to drink

I've caught the tears the were dripping

down your beautiful lash

I pressed my lips up to the glass

God can only count my last breaths

I cry for my lover's breasts
I was blinded by love
in the face of death

Dead Stars

The shine
of the stars
have been dead
for many years

In the same way
I feel you
but you're not
really here

Ocean Blue

Sailing on a ocean of new love
is only hopelessly drifting of true love

That place where you first set sail
that place when you told a grand tail

A simple wave
a complex wind
a compass that cannot spin

As you go along the blue
you forgot about your crew

Lost in-between
the seven seas
If I can only make
you believe

That the stars lead me to you

My ocean blue

Each Step

That day all the pain went away
walking up your stairs
showed how much I really cared

Each step I gave you my soul
each floor I painfully endured

Open the door to be adored

Hearts implode
love explodes
body's exposed

Hot flesh yearning
tension burning
through your perfection
our future had a connection

lets go back to the start
where our love first sparked

Every Curve

Clothes get in the way of your curves
Clothes get in the way of my nerves
pressed against every single
one of your nerves;
Clothes take to long
To show you what your
Body truly deserves.
The way my fingers
can drift and swerve;
My words will become Verbs
I will travel the skin of your universe

Let us dive into the sea
We will dance & scream

I can't give you what you've always wanted
I can only give you what you've always dreamed

Are you tired of empty nights
Nothing in this world worth the fight

I can only give you what you've always dreamed;
a moment to finally be free
I know the real you, not the girl the mirror only see's
God will love you
even if you don't believe

Dive into the sea
Off the shore
Tell me you didn't love
when I took off
your high
wasted shorts.

You're simply breath taking
you take the death out of me
the sun reflects crystals off the sea
a glimpse into your heart
I see such beautiful things
I believe in miracles
every time
your smile sings

You're simply breath taking
your reflection must make you faint
your passion is fueled by love & strength

I'm afraid when I lay you across my bed
that I don't deserve your grace
because you're an angel only god can create
&
I will spend my life
to your existence
no matter what it takes

I understand the pain
I remember the rain
but don't feel so ashamed
you're a beautiful girl
you have so much to gain

I hope this pen and paper
brings me fame
So I can tell the entire world
your name;

That every drop of ink
dips into my drink
changing the way I think
slowly making my heart sink
I see you when I close my eyes
just not when I blink;

Every line I ever wrote
no words could ever express
this feeling of hope

Melting stars through my telescope
rushing streams
down the freckles
of your throat

Remember
the
words
of
truth
I
spoke

I sleep to wake

"Sorry I didn't mean to wake you"

Don't be sorry, I don't mind
waking in your presence
& sleeping in your
absence

All I knew

I couldn't understand
what you were saying

All I knew was that
every time you
opened your mouth

All the boys
listened

Never mistake love for lust
But what if I am deeply in love with your lust
& hopelessly in lust with your love;
My bones shall decay into dust
In attempt to sow the stars into a blanket for us

I have never tasted
a drop of rum
without the touch of you
beneath my tongue.
I'm drunk before
the nights begun
the moonlight
rises my demons
My heart must overcome;

I'm to old
to feel this young
I wrote you
a million
poems
&
you
never
even
read

One

When a diamond is being created
it's under so much pressure
in order give forth a dazzling treasure
So much struggle and heat
it must fight to overcome defeat
remember when Jesus
washed sinners feet;

No matter how long the waves crash
upon the ocean shore
the sand stands strong to the earths very core
each grain of sand every drop of water
I find myself back at your door
wanting oh so much more;
My body's getting weary
I'm force to sink below
sink down under to the
depths of the ocean floor;

As my mind starts to drift
I reminisce a time when
the rum was thick
a time when life wasn't a bitch
a moment when the clock didn't tick
a feeling of love when I kissed your lips
My breath is nearly gone
my memoirs can only last for oh so long
the sun is reaching dawn I cry for
the world as my pearl slips from my palms
love is never gone just the beautiful voice
that once sang our song

There was once a time
when the sunlight
spilled through the blinds
&
at that moment
you were
truly
truly
mine

Where I didn't
suffocate
in your presence
The essential of
your essence left
a intoxicated resent
of your fragrance
How can something
so magnificent
be nonexistent

I'm reaching for you in my dreams
grasping you in my nightmares
distance beyond measure
by what we had here

One night I swear to God
I honestly believed
I felt your skin
& I indulge in reminisce
what is was like to
breath again

Before
I could
fall over
the waterfall
beyond the horizon

I crashed my ship
on your reef
Marooned by my love
of the sea

I was forced
to burn my ship
the warmth
of your tongue
was my scripture
but your only gave me a lick;
Mermaids lurk,
trying to see where in
my heart they can fit,
there hair tangles my sails
the salt on there skin
it breaths–it inhales
The way my body moves to
the rhythm of there tails

My
dreams
are a
mere
fairytale
your love
is my youth

My holy grail

The ink drips down

the S & the E
& after the X

I dream of what's next
your hot beautiful sex

Feel the motion of my pen
Satisfy your every desire
As the screams get higher

Listening to the breaths
between the moans;
the rain dripping between
the beats of my heart
&
the writings
I've never shown

The ink of your sex
drips down my biceps

I was here before you were born
I'll be here after your dead
I'll be the promises broken
& the promises kept;

I reminisce the day we met
...
Do you still smell the flowers
I had always left at your doorstep

We ate cereal to our
favorite cartoons
We made love
every afternoon
We drank on roof tops
& danced with the moon
I saw your smile
from across the room
I was Infatuated
by your perfume

You came over
pulled me close
& said...

"I don't have a curfew
imagine all the things
that we could do"

That night we raised
our glasses to the moon
& Every night since
Was our honeymoon

Enquire

Just because
I hate you more
does not mean
I love you
any less

I was so blessed
to undress
your
beautiful
success

Careless every sin of your flesh
lay your past & forget your stress

My life's meaning
is to excess
your being

My heart requires
your happiest desires
only God can conspire
a love I can never Enquire

Vinyl

I want to place
my needle
on the vinyl
of your skin

Hear the music
as we let it spin

Withdrawals

Open the space
embrace the taste
biting your nails
enjoying the pace
remember that place
I laid you down
that place I kneed &
gave you my crown

You grasped my shoulders
and screamed without a sound
I kissed every drop that
was dripping down

Your body was
a waterfall
poring over
my withdrawals

Just let me

I fell in love with both eyes open
but stayed in love with one eye closed
what I remember the most
is fighting the final dose
seeping through my veins
Bursting out in pain
heart draining in shame
from you not feeling the same
You became the heat burning my flame

Be my cherry on top

melt the sweetness as it drips off

You're

so sexy

So baby

just let me

Endlessly

It's just a feeling that I have
I skip a beat when our eyes meet;
when your hair falls upon your face
I understood what god meant by grace;
I'm captured by the photos you create
that develop the darkest parts of my faith
endless fine lines undress my demise
simply trace your lovely sublime
drunk off your body
spilling the corona & lime
just hold my hand
& we'll drift
endlessly through time

Felt the vibe

Your true colors got thrown in
with my whites.
Thrown together by mixed emotions
& bad advice

My words fell empty that night
&
You proved my doubts right;
Have fun burning your life
In the limelight
& you pull some bullshit by saying
"Your nice but it just isn't right"

Tell me, when was the last time
You let your heart decide
Took off your shoes & had a dance
Felt the vibe without
getting fucked in a trance

Same sky

I mat not be
able to sleep
with you in
the same bed
but
I'm sleeping
under the
same sky
&
that's all I need

Have mine

If
there
ever
comes
a day
when
you
can
no
longer
smile

You
can
always
have
mine

Hoping fences

We always got a little tipsy
& right through the bottle
I saw your soul
how beautify misty

The nights got so wild
The way the moon smiled
We hoped every fence as far as a mile

Remember how your locks
got tangled in the highest fence
As I untangle it,
I softly said
"I love you now; I loved you then
you belong stretch out across my bed"

Every night that I drink & hop a fence
I reminisce your ear echoing my heartbeat
through my chest

I Taught You

Drips upon your lips
making love to those hips
lust combusts
trust retouched

Body's open
hearts broken
skin
peeling
feelings
reeling

Back against the wall
When you go down
I fall
In love with you
Doing the things
I taught
you
to
do

The Tattoos I Never Knew

Right between your hips
Is where my figure perfectly fits
Where all ink streams
Down the crevices of your lips

I fucked you to Kendrick
Made love to Hendrix

I miss you right now
Beyond the distance
Tattoos are all the same
But ours were different

In-Between

There's no drink or drug

to ever replace

your warm hug

Love begins

Love ends

somewhere

In-between

You're still
My Best Friend

My backs against the wall
just hearing your call
reminds me of all the
fighting throughout the halls

The floor to your door
pours my soul upon your core
you tore, you adore

Our hearts apart
if we never end
then when do we start

I cried
you complained
left with
just a goodbye

God only knows the pain
when I must replace
the face
that traces
to the places
when I walk those
Staircases

Parking Lots

Close the car
turn the locks

The Moonlight gleamed
as you took off your top

Lips sank as the
windows dripped hot
I was young
making love
in paking lots

Through My Will

I look through her eyes
but it brings me back to yours

Rain pours as I'm counting my steps
back to your door

You asked for my heart so politely
I gave it ever so lightly

Love what you have
not have what you love

It was not into my ear
you whispered
but into my heart
It was not my lips
that you kissed
but my soul
that you
blissfully
split

I love you through my will
till the sun grows cold
till the stars get old

Starting at forever
ending at never

Masterpiece

God created you
then god created me
he molded our souls
into a masterpiece

My Ink

This pen
represents
my tongue
this paper your skin
now lets dip my ink
& let us begin

Ghost

What is my name
If you meant it
the most

I keep seeing you
but it's only
a ghost

Love & Bone

The way God wrote
his love on pages
& stone

The same way
you write
your love
on my
flesh and bone

If I knew, that day would be the last time I'd see you

I would have held you with no fear

If I knew, that day would be the last time I'd see you

I would have kissed you & wiped your tear

If I knew, that day would be the last time I'd see you

I would have told you I loved you cause you're the only song I hear

My Juliet My Daisy

I believed I was your Romeo
And you were my Juliet
That we'll die together
By the blissful sunset

But you were my Daisy
So I died by the sea
Alone like Gatsby

Only Thing

I asked God
"When is it over"

When their memories
are the only thing
Giving you closure

We knew this day was coming
that's why we were running
trying to outrun the rising sun
listening to your heart hum
feel the rhythm of my tongue

Among my dreams
are pulling apart at the seams
drowning down a rushing stream
screaming to breathe your themes

If your feeling down
you can always
turn around

My mind is so pretensions
to the words you once mention
our minds full of tension
our hearts crying for attention

The less of your dress
expresses the senses of your skin
I'm spinning where you begin
Fuses are burning thin

Remembering the blur
reminiscing your curves
since I love you
I'll take it on the chin
take all your pain
from within

I wasn't happy about our mad situation
you don't know the frustration
going back & forth
at the train stations

Weekend after weekend of sensation
waiting alone at bus stations
to get in your bed
for some temptations

You left me in a pool
of tears and hopes
you cut the rope
that we made
once upon a time ago

But I did not fall
walked straight down that hall
saw each step & looked back for a sec
you looked so beautiful the day we met
you forced me to leave
but never forget

You could be anything you want to be
but you choose to sit here and sing with me;
After all the songs we already sung
you still burn me like the morning sun;
The songs of yesterday's
are always here to stay
Your hair wraps through my mind
as your bangs tangled all the songs I sang
I sang, I sang I felt those bangs
they were the reason
my soul sank

Breath you in
when I want you out
I hold my breath
but my heart it shouts
I'll tell you I miss you &
I don't know how
I never heard silence
quit this loud

Her & The Universe

You're the surface in my universe
the melody to my verse
the water to my thirst
the scares alongside the hurt
you're the purpose to my universe;
a seed was planted in this ancient earth
this cosmic dirt
grew our love
& gave birth
to this
colorful
magnificent
gorgeous
universe

Letters

I remember

your Birthday

but forgot

your age

I wrote you

A hundred letters

now lets

turn the
page

Remember the tears that you shed
that made your heart bled

I'll never forget the way
we laid upon our bed

I rest my head on your chest
kissing your flesh
love is merely
Gods test;
Praying for the best
so much regrets
things left unsaid
Lights so dim
feeling of your skin
drops of love down your chin
biting the pain
thrusting away
I cry for that day
I miss the way we use to sway

Woman have been all I've ever known
my body was born of one
my soul capture by some
when my heart grew num
when songs are no longer sung
when life is finally done
when death has ultimately won

My last breath was taken
when I was young
& it shall be taken again

My mind was stone
my eyes like doves

A woman was the
rushing of my blood

My last breath will utter

"My Love"

My pen showed our chemistry
Erase the flowing of ink
Imagine if you cannot think

That first date
is when my book
went open wide
when blank pages became
a canvas of our art
painting why we fell apart

where my brushes
remember your touch
I kissed you &
made the
noise hush

I can hear
the voice
that made
the choice
to paint
those stars
to always
love you
for
who you are

I see Gods colors
in the way I felt
the way we melt
the way it dripped and dropped
into the hour glass of time

You poured it &
made it un-wined
peel the lie
undress the truth
give me a taste
of what is you

Swing back and forth on the tress of spring
showering how the flowers came to be

Hour after hour of sorrow
when did goodbye
blow the sands of tomorrow
God gave this life to only borrow

I should have heard the underline tone
the wind I felt in my bones
On a friday night
I'm left alone
to muse over
your lovely moan

The Morning
& her

It was by the garden you were taking in your favorite roses.
I couldn't help but always follow her here quietly through the night where the
moon was off beyond the stars & there was nothing to escape the darkness.
The only vibrant girl of the entire universe was handed down with such
exquisiteness & symmetry of elegance. I was blessed to be a man in that
moment to be marveled by the sun giving birth; To be here & now witnessing
love in its proper form, dancing across the meadow shinning like sunlight
through God's Window. I was struck like never before or never to be again; of all
that is perfect I hadn't fallen in love with her, I had fallen in love with her dress,
her music, her ability to wake with the morning calm, I had fallen in love with
the earth she walked on; & as she smelled the faint aroma of the roses
She looked up & noticed me secretly looking at her from across the garden

All she had done was smiled & went her way forever as my unforgiving muse

One evening like any other
I got this uneasy feeling.
A blend of gratifying
mixed emotions
rushed into me

At a distance I knew,
even before seeing what she
honestly looked like.
That I was going to be writing
a great deal of hopeless poems
about her loveliness she poured out.

she walked into my existence with
her mind straight & body cured.
Vibrant hair that fell over,
brushing her creamy cheeks,
barely touching her malleable complexion.
A dress that melted over her skin
that made me fall beyond in love with her

Over the cloak of her masquerade
was a glamour,
that fashion designers were consisting
trying to make happen;
but her & her alone
created fashion with a fade of grace

When she got naked
she didn't undress herself
she undressed my soul

I found her at a café
I've seen her here once before
sipping on rose coloured wine

Sitting alone, I might add
wondrous. mysterious
I could tell that her eyes
were a bit different. this time

All the styles of her hair,
how it waterfalled down;
gently over
her dimples
that sank into her lower back,
The jewelry that hung over
her breathless chest.
all the rings that wrapped
around her fingers
just like how she had me.
almost like sugar was
being poured over her flawless skin

A sweet taste cascaded briskly into my lungs
of a complex mixture
of lust, smoke & perfume.
seamlessly she knew
all the things she had done to me
not to mention other men

The year was 1920.

I was in a state of being a young gentleman among the streets of Paris.
with the night at my back & a suit to cover my front,
I could wash down this town like a glass of fine champagne.
toward the nights wild end, I stumbled upon a small cafe
a little ways down from a one-night in cheap hotel.

woman came & went from this place but one stood out from the rest,
laying her elbows on the bar; smoking the ashes of her past.
she was reading vogue,
I could tell she had a fashion sense just by the way she filled the room.

"Pardon me darling, may I indulge in the rest of the evening with you"

"Why of course chéri, **come sit...sit"**

"Bonjour belle, my name is Brandon"

**"Bonjour monsieur Brandon, my God you're beau.
It is a pleasure; My name is Coco...Coco Chanel"**

That night we talked until they brought us the morning menus.
she took off her pretty little shoes; stood up, gave me a kiss on the cheek
& said **"I enjoy your writings, I oh so much do. Wild cards like us
will die in this dreadful world but live forever in our passions;
stay handsome babe"**

Then she left me there with a red stained kiss
& a perfume that dissented forever into my poems,

many years later
my little girl would be begging me to buy her clothes

It was only in intoxicating
moments that I ultimately
knew, if she didn't come
home with me that night.
I would never get a chance
to end her misery
& begin my happiness

We could fade away into the
drinks that were to strong
for our weak spirits

It was an off gesture
that undoubtedly caught my eye,
she was so attracted to me
she tried hiding it like a secret never told.
She subconsciously lost her cool;
looking away taking a desperate sip of her drink.
No one notice but my obsessed self,
She was far to breath taking in a dress;
she had her shots strong & her men smooth.

I didn't know what to make of her,
All I wanted all I honestly needed
was one minute to confess everything
every guy never had the guts to say.

So I took a shot in the dark &
for all my days to come
party's weren't so lonely

The moon had been late
for a very important date

Your smile was so inviting,
just by the way her lips enclosed
the glass of her refreshment
was appealing; by far beautiful

An awakening comic essence
lingered over of drinks of choice

She had the champagne
& I indulge in the whiskey

The very fabric of the moment of her
was the most magnificent thing
this divine earth had ever witnessed;

A girl with a fine glass
of whatever she desired
& a cigarette with
some boy to light it
was all a girl really needed

I felt as if she could see past
our conversations,
through my hopeful thoughts of her
wrapped in-between my sheets.
She wasn't even talking; just starring
waiting for me to say something exciting
like

"The next train for Paris
leaves a stroke past midnight
let's catch it"

The shower was a place
for just me & you

A place where the truth was naked,
the laughter was soaked &
the passion was drenched in steam

The rain was to cold;
so we hugged
in warm tears
until our fingers got pruney

All we did
was let the water
run down our skin

your hair was thick & wet
my kisses covered
more of your body
than water droplets

As water fell, so did I

As the drain took our water away
so did you

It always astonishes me the things girls

put up with for the mere sake of acceptance.

I'm not one to say I can truly meet every girls fancy but what's desperately unfair is

Men who think they're entitled to a woman's physique, like it's never been hers.

Somehow these foolish men have come to the conclusion that their eyes have molded

their endless curves & admirable angelic angel hair.

As if there own hands can really feel her untouchable animate beauty.

Ever since my bones have grow into what they're now, courageous & strong.

I've known that is order to really, truley, romantically convey her needs

You Must Love God.

For he crafted her soul with galaxies

her smile with rainbows

her dimples with falling stars

her fingers tips with pools of heaven

& her eye's with moon dust mixed up

with a piece of God's personal poetry

Our fates always met at midnight,
In a small timeless Paris café
Where the moonlight spilled through the blind
& at the end of every table was a character worth buying a drink.

She was there, opposite of me
with a presence only music could match

Hours became moments,
words became strings
that held us together,
Her drinks were straight
nothing like her path in life

I had this unparallel feeling,
not only. Did I want her
to escape with me;
I wanted to drink all night until we were forced to get
married...not with each other but this hazy café

The bartender would be the priest
& the everyone would cheer! in awe;

This café gave us our first laugh,
Our first unforgettable night,
Our first time truly alive,
The first time I knew what was real &
The first & last moment an hour
could be so full of sweetness

We took a stroll before the sun took her away
her lungs| must have been a dragon's
from how much she smoked
&
As the city lit up
Our cigarettes did the same

She often glanced out her bedside window,
looking over the city; taking in the sounds &
breathing in it's history;
All she ever wanted was to run the streets
with a song to sing, hop fences with no one chasing her
& I guess you could say
feel as high as the skyscrapers
she was to wild to be in

Describe love;

Her laughter.

Describe hate;

Silence.

All the woman were
blossoming their jewelry
like flower pedals dancing
hand in hand with their
promising reflections

I guess we'll always be
oil & vinegar
we go together
but
we just don't mix

I am
Thankful
for you
giving me
something
you can never
get back

"What?"

Your time.

It was one thing to wait for
someone to get ready,
but waiting for her to glance
back across a distant scene;
beyond doubt was testing my
patience with god

It was something about a woman in the morning
that became my belief in forever

How the sun traveled such a great distance
just to touch her tangled hair,
before I had the pleasure
to wrap it around my fingers

It was something about a woman in the morning;
Just the way life played it's melody
of sweet tender music between her sheets.

She stood up from the bed
& walked over to the bathroom.
There she looked into the mirror with
the same look in her eyes the night we first kissed

She looked deeply
no make-up
no dress
no one
but me staring across
laying on the bed.

"I love us," she said

"I love us, together not apart &
If we are ever apart I hope we fall back together;
I don't love you & you don't love me

We both love us."

The last bottle we shared together
was still sitting here beside my bed
there was one drop left
hoping you'll come back & finish it

Sometimes

Goodbye

is

the

best

way

to

say

I

Love

You

Made in the USA
San Bernardino, CA
02 October 2013